SNOWBOARDING

SNOWBOARDING

ODYSSEYS

JIM WHITING

CREATIVE EDUCATION · CREATIVE PAPERBACKS

Published by Creative Education and Creative Paperbacks
P.O. Box 227, Mankato, Minnesota 56002
Creative Education and Creative Paperbacks
are imprints of The Creative Company
www.thecreativecompany.us

Design by Blue Design (www.bluedes.com)
Production by Joe Kahnke
Art direction by Rita Marshall
Printed in China

Photographs by Alamy (Accent Alaska.com, jackrcoyne/
Stockimo, PA Images, Ricardo Ribas), The Enthusiast Network
(Alex Williams/Snowboarder Magazine), Getty Images
(FABRICE COFFRINI/AFP, JOE KLAMAR/AFP, Daniel Milchev/
Stone, Tom Pennington/Getty Images Sport, Doug Pensinger/
Getty Images Sport, JAVIER SORIANO/AFP, Cameron
Spencer/Getty Images Sport), iStockphoto (Creativaimages,
Soren Hald, ultramarinfoto), Newscom (Kyodo), Shutterstock
(Lukas Gojda, Hekla, IM_photo, Ipatov, Samot, Sorbis, Dmytro
Vietrov)

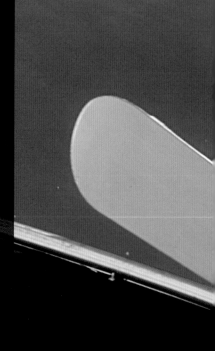

Library of Congress Cataloging-in-Publication Data
Names: Whiting, Jim, author.
Title: Snowboarding / Jim Whiting.
Series: Odysseys in extreme sports.
Includes bibliographical references and index.
Summary: An in-depth survey of the popular extreme sport of
snowboarding, from its Michigan roots to its current Olympic
presence, as well as its techniques, records, equipment, and
famous boarders.
Identifiers: LCCN 2017028051 / ISBN 978-1-60818-696-9
(hardcover) / ISBN 978-1-62832-292-7 (pbk) / ISBN 978-1-
56660-732-2 (eBook)

Subjects: LCSH: Snowboarding—Juvenile literature.
Classification: LCC GV857.S57 W5575 2018 / DDC 796.939—
dc23

CCSS: RI 8.1, 2, 3, 4, 5, 8, 10; RI 9-10.1, 2, 3, 4, 5, 8, 10; RI 11-12.1,
2, 3, 4, 5, 10; RST 6-8.1, 2, 5, 6, 10; RST 9-10.1, 2, 5, 6, 10; RST
11-12.1, 2, 5, 6, 10

First Edition HC 9 8 7 6 5 4 3 2 1
First Edition PBK 9 8 7 6 5 4 3 2 1

CONTENTS

Introduction

Soured on soccer? Fed up with football? Bored by baseball? Turned off by team sports? If so, extreme sports might be more to your liking. While there's not an exact definition of what makes a sport "extreme," the following characteristics (or at least most of them) seem to be common: a higher degree of risk despite use of protective gear, emphasis on achieving high speeds and/or

OPPOSITE: During the early years of snowboarding, the sport was dominated by thrill-seeking boys and young men. Today, boarders of all ages and skill levels hit the slopes to enjoy this winter activity.

heights, more likely to be performed alone or with a handful of friends, no issues with playing time as in team sports, stunts requiring substantial amounts of skill and practice, less emphasis on formal rules, and an adrenaline rush from physical exertion.

For many people, hurtling downhill on a snowy slope with the icy wind blowing in their faces is the ultimate thrill. For years, getting that rush meant skiing, sledding, or sitting on something like an inner tube, lunch tray, or chunk of cardboard. Starting in the mid-1960s, another option emerged: You could stand on a board with the same shape as its larger cousin, the surfboard. And you could do the same sort of tricks as a skateboarder. It not only had the same sort of anti-establishment edge as those other board sports, it also gave their riders something to do in the winter months. Snowboarding was born.

Snurfin' Safari

Unlike most sports, games, and activities, the origins of snowboarding can be pinpointed almost to the hour. Snowboarding began on Christmas morning in 1965 in the city of Muskegon, Michigan. Sherman and Nancy Poppen and their two daughters had opened their presents. Nancy, pregnant with the couple's third child, asked her husband to take the two girls outside and do something with them so that she could rest.

Poppen already had several inventions to his credit, so his mind quickly went into high gear. He spotted a pair of three-foot-long (0.9 m) skis still encased in their bubble packaging. He hammered a couple of pieces of wood to connect them. He and the girls went out into their yard, which had a gentle slope. The crosspieces provided something for them to brace their feet against as they stood on the board and glided down the hill. Neighbor kids saw what was happening and soon were sharing time on the new toy with Poppen's girls.

"When I saw how much fun the kids had Christmas Day," Poppen said, "I spent the next week in Goodwill and everywhere else buying up every water ski I could find." His next move was attaching a rope to the front of the board. It not only provided a measure of control but also kept the board from sliding down the slope in the event of a fall.

As Poppen thought about his invention, he realized that it combined elements of several summer-oriented sports: surfing, slalom waterskiing, and skateboarding. When he mentioned his thoughts to his wife, she came up with a name for it: snurfer, a combination of "snow" and "surfer."

Poppen patented the snurfer, then licensed it to Brunswick, a leading sporting goods manufacturer. Soon, the first snurfers were being mass-produced. The company ran ads reading "Snurfing! The greatest word in downhill fun with the thrills of skiing and the skills of surfing." During the following decade, the company sold about a million snurfers.

In the meantime, several people were beginning to make what were eventually called snowboards. Chief among them were Tom Sims, who founded SIMS® in 1976, and Jake Burton Carpenter (better known as Jake Burton), who formed his own company the following year. They began a commercial rivalry that helped push snowboarding into the national consciousness and resulted in numerous innovations that improved the quality of the sport.

Perhaps the most important were bindings. They gave boarders much more control. Burton is often credited with introducing them at a snurfing competition in 1979. The other participants objected because the bindings and the design of his board were considerably different from their own snurfers. Organizers had to create a separate category for him. It didn't take long for everyone to see the advantages that Burton's innovation offered. As Canadian pro boarder Ross Rebagliati points

out, "It may or may not be a coincidence that Brunswick stopped making snurfers later that year."

However, a problem soon emerged. Hardly any established ski areas would allow snowboarders to use their facilities. Ski areas weren't covered by insurance if something happened to snowboarders using their facilities. In addition, people weren't used to being around the typically young and edgy snowboarders. They didn't fit in with the traditional skiers. To help everyone become more comfortable, snowboard manufacturers began visiting ski areas, demonstrating their boards and pointing out the advantages of allowing boarders to use their slopes. As the sport gained more participants, resistance gradually crumbled. In a little more than a decade, snowboarding became accepted in hundreds of ski resorts throughout the country.

Another factor in the growing acceptance of the sport was the first magazine devoted to snowboarding. Called *Absolutely Radical* in its first issue in March 1985, the publication changed its name to the more descriptive *International Snowboard Magazine*. "It told real stories from the early days without embellishment," said long-time winter sports photographer Bud Fawcett. "It was the original source of information from the contest scene which was driving the sport for so long in the 1980s."

A key snowboarding development came in 1990.

For several years, ski areas had tried to make their own half-pipes by hand. The method was slow and difficult, with uneven results. So a Colorado farmer named Doug Waugh invented the Pipe Dragon. It was a converted farm machine that quickly and easily carved out half-pipes. Half-pipes, in turn, attracted more boarders.

n the summer of 1995, the ESPN cable sports network showcased the talents of extreme athletes in the first X Games. The event proved so popular that a winter version debuted in 1997. Snowboarding was one of the featured sports.

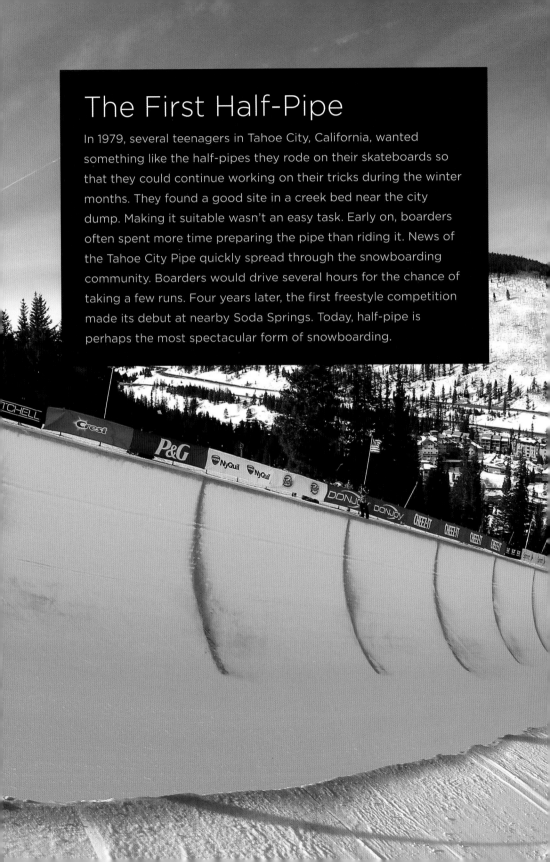

The First Half-Pipe

In 1979, several teenagers in Tahoe City, California, wanted something like the half-pipes they rode on their skateboards so that they could continue working on their tricks during the winter months. They found a good site in a creek bed near the city dump. Making it suitable wasn't an easy task. Early on, boarders often spent more time preparing the pipe than riding it. News of the Tahoe City Pipe quickly spread through the snowboarding community. Boarders would drive several hours for the chance of taking a few runs. Four years later, the first freestyle competition made its debut at nearby Soda Springs. Today, half-pipe is perhaps the most spectacular form of snowboarding.

The following year, snowboarding was introduced into the Winter Olympics in Nagano, Japan. Men and women competed in the parallel giant slalom and half-pipe events, and 22 nations had entrants. After winning two bronze medals that year, United States athletes dominated the medal count at the next Winter Games. In Salt Lake City, Utah, Ross Powers led a sweep of the men's half-pipe and Kelly Clark took the women's half-pipe gold. Snowboarding proved so popular that snowboard cross, a downhill race with six boarders at a time, was added in 2006. Two more events—parallel slalom and slopestyle—debuted in Sochi, Russia, in 2014. Illustrating snowboarding's now worldwide popularity, athletes from 14 countries took medals. Americans topped the list with three golds and a pair of bronzes.

In the early 2000s, a charismatic young boarder

named Shaun White further energized the sport. Nicknamed the "Flying Tomato" because of his bright red hair, White has won more than a dozen gold medals at the Winter X Games since 2003, as well as Winter Olympic gold medals in 2006, 2010, and 2018. His first Olympic gold medal capped a season in which he had won several Grand Prix Olympic Qualifiers and two Winter X Games events. He also enjoyed his first-ever wins at the U.S. Open that year, topping the list in both half-pipe and slopestyle.

Gearing Up and Gliding Down

There are three primary divisions of snowboarding: freeriding, racing, and freestyle. Each has a board type to match. Freeriding—also known as all-mountain—is the most widespread. It's just you and your board (and maybe a few buddies) going down established trails or breaking new ground. Freeriding boards account for more than half of all sales. They are directional, which means that they

OPPOSITE: Snowboards are available in many sizes and shapes and for different purposes. Be sure to talk to an expert before buying one.

are meant to be ridden in one direction. The board is widest at the nose and tail, tapering slightly to the middle.

Racing obviously involves getting down the hill as fast as possible. You may race independently, with the winner determined by the fastest time. Or you and another person may start at the same time, with the first to the bottom declared as the winner. In snowboard cross racing, as many as six people start simultaneously and negotiate the turns and bumps of the hill as they seek to be the first across the finish line. Racing boards are

longer and narrower than most other boards.

Freestyle is where boarders get to show off their bag of tricks. Freestyle boards are shorter and wider than other boards. They are also lighter in weight and more flexible. While they are easier to turn, they don't go as fast as racing boards.

G etting started in snowboarding can seem especially daunting. There are so many choices to make, from the board itself to clothing and accessories. Your board will be the most important purchase. It's a

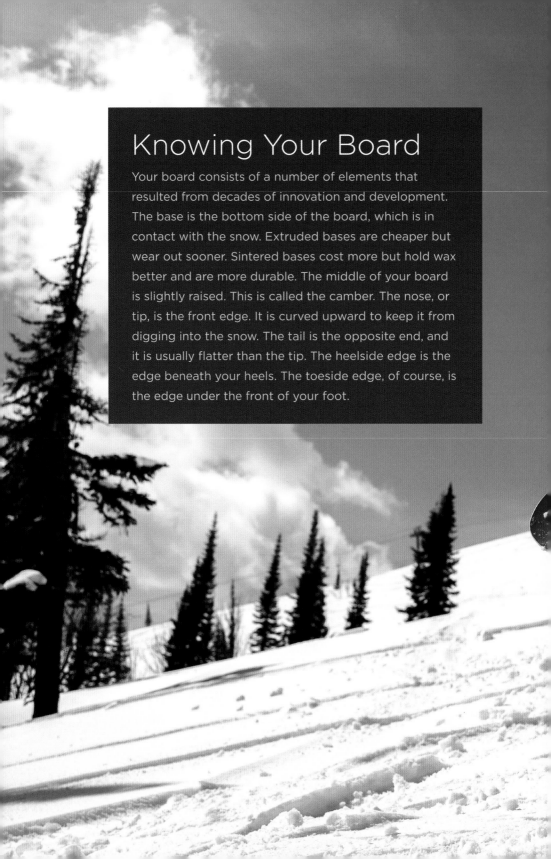

Knowing Your Board

Your board consists of a number of elements that resulted from decades of innovation and development. The base is the bottom side of the board, which is in contact with the snow. Extruded bases are cheaper but wear out sooner. Sintered bases cost more but hold wax better and are more durable. The middle of your board is slightly raised. This is called the camber. The nose, or tip, is the front edge. It is curved upward to keep it from digging into the snow. The tail is the opposite end, and it is usually flatter than the tip. The heelside edge is the edge beneath your heels. The toeside edge, of course, is the edge under the front of your foot.

good idea to learn as much as possible beforehand by reading books and checking out websites. You might also consider renting equipment on your first visits to the slopes.

Mountain weather can quickly change, so you need to be prepared for a wide variety of conditions. Experts recommend layering, starting with a couple of lightweight garments that don't absorb sweat or other moisture. Top those with a waterproof jacket and pants. Cotton is not a good choice for layering. It becomes waterlogged when wet. Thin wool is better because it still retains warmth if it becomes damp. Synthetic fabrics are also good because they wick away moisture. The jacket should be long enough to cover your rear end. Extra padding on the knees and back side of the pants will lessen the impact from falling.

Many experts maintain that boots are the most vital part of your equipment. They need to be snug but not tight because you'll be wearing them for many hours. All snowboarding boots have a soft liner, which provides stability and cushioning. You can pay extra for a custom-fit liner. Flex is another consideration in buying boots. Beginners are usually better off with a softer flex because it is more forgiving. As you gain experience, you'll usually want a stiffer flex. And be sure to get a few pairs of snowboard-specific socks. Synthetic and wool are the best choices here.

Bindings are the next piece of equipment to consider. In general, bindings conform to the three types of boarding. All-mountain bindings are the best choice for beginners because they are the most versatile. Bindings are also made to fit with the amount of flex of your boots.

The most common is strap-in. One strap goes across the toe of your boot and the other around the ankle. The third type is rear-entry, also known as "speed entry." A hinged, high back folds down, you insert your boot, then fold the back up and you're ready to go.

As with nearly all extreme sports, a helmet is vital to protect your head. Like your boots, it should be snug but not overly tight, since you'll likely be wearing it for long periods. Helmets have a hard plastic outer shell plus an inner liner made of foam. This inner liner is designed to absorb the impact from a collision and should be replaced after a serious fall. Vents allow cool air to enter and to wick away moisture to prevent overheating. Some helmets have detachable ear pads and liners. You can also get helmets equipped with built-in speakers and cameras or detachable camera mounts.

Snowboarders need eye protection in the form of sunglasses or tinted goggles. These goggles often come with interchangeable lenses to adapt to changing weather conditions on the slope.

Once you're suitably equipped, it's time to start learning to ride. Remember to take things slow and easy. You should feel completely comfortable in one phase before moving on to the next.

Because falling is a certainty, especially in the early stages, learning how to fall is a good place to start. There

are actually several different ways to fall, depending on the position of your board when you lose your balance. Relaxation is one key to surviving a fall. Another is learning hand and arm placement to reduce the chances of a break or strain. You also need to learn how to get back up without wasting too much energy.

Then you'll learn the basic riding position. Your front arm is pointed in the direction you want to take, with your upper body rotated a little in the same direction. Your back arm is slightly bent. Flex your front knee slightly to act as a shock absorber and put most of your weight on it while keeping your back leg relaxed.

From this position, you'll learn the basic moves as well as keeping your board under control. Again, always stay well within your comfort zone. Start with very gentle slopes and gradually increase the angle of the incline.

The next step is learning how to turn. Once you've mastered single turns, you link them together. Now you're ready to move on to carving. That means you use the edge of the board to cut a line into the snow as you turn. This is where you start to lean into the turn, sometimes going so far to the side that your hand goes into the snow.

Congratulations! You're on your way to enjoying one of the world's most exhilarating sports.

Turn, Baby, Turn!

The key to turning is shifting your weight to different parts of the board during the maneuver. Don't hurry. Make each movement slowly and carefully. In a heelside turn, begin by turning your head and upper body in the direction you want to travel. Apply pressure onto your toe edge with your knees bent. Shift your weight forward to point downhill. As you accelerate, rise up a little, extend your arms forward and upward, and allow the board to flatten out. Still keeping your arms up, apply pressure on the heel edge with your front foot. As the rest of the board settles onto the heel edge, turn your head and upper body in the new direction and bend your knees.

Big-Name Boarders

Jake Burton is generally regarded as the most influential figure in the development and ongoing popularity of snowboarding. He got his first snurfer as a Christmas present when he was 14. While attending the University of Colorado, he turned to competitive skiing. His racing career was cut short by a serious automobile accident, though. He returned home to New York and graduated from college in 1977 with an economics degree.

OPPOSITE: Jake Burton's first Burton Boards featured bindings and a rope with a handle. Now one of the largest snowboard retailers, Burton's company also sells accessories and winter gear.

He went to work for a finance company but soon realized the job wasn't for him. Though he knew very little about woodworking, he moved to Vermont and started a small snowboard manufacturing company called Burton Boards. He began making prototypes and testing them in the nearby mountains.

He finally settled on a model called the Burton Backhill. But it sold so poorly that Jake had to lay off his entire staff. He refused to quit, though. "From the word go, Jake understood that snowboarding represented the future of the snow-resort industry," Ross Rebagliati observes. "Before there was even a viable market for snowboards, he was creating snowboard events, he was starting up snowboard camps, and he was financing the research and development of snowboarding equipment." Introducing bindings and soft boots were just two of his innovations. Today, Burton Snowboards is one of the world's largest snowboard manufacturers.

Jake never loses sight of the purpose of his boards: having fun. "If it snows two feet the night before, we understand there are going to be a lot of empty desks the next morning," he says of his employees. "The large majority of people can probably find a way to ride a few hours, come in, and work a few hours late."

s a long-time advocate of the sport, Burton has influenced the peak of snowboarding per-

The U.S. Open Championships

In 1982, Paul Graves—one of snurfing's earliest "big names"—organized the first National Snow Surfing Championships at Vermont's Suicide Six ski resort. Nearly 200 people turned out to compete. They wore everything from jeans and running shoes to hiking boots and one-piece snowsuits. The starting gate was an upside-down kitchen table. Competitors used its legs as leverage to zoom downhill at speeds of more than 50 miles (80.5 km) per hour. The event gained national recognition on NBC's *Today*, most likely because it seemed so offbeat. Jake Burton took over the event the next year. Now known as the Burton U.S. Open Snowboarding Championships, it is held in Vail, Colorado, where it attracts up to 30,000 spectators.

formance, the Winter Olympic Games. Foremost among Olympic snowboarding medalists is Shaun White. For many people, snowboarding is synonymous with him. White took up skiing at the age of four and snowboarding two years later. Within a year, he received his first sponsorship. When he wasn't on the slopes, he was skateboarding. Noted skateboarder Tony Hawk took 9-year-old White under his wing and White turned pro in that sport at the age of 17.

But it's thanks to snowboarding that the Flying Tomato has received most of his fame. From 2003 to 2015, he won 13 gold medals in the Winter X Games, along with 3 silvers and a pair of bronzes.

On the world's largest sporting stage, the heavily favored White won the half-pipe at both the 2006 and 2010 Winter Olympics. But in one of the most stunning

Legendary snowboarder Shaun White took the gold in men's half-pipe in the 2006 and 2010 Olympic Games, but a fall during the 2014 event kept him from winning another medal.

outcomes in Olympic history, he didn't even medal at the 2014 Olympics. He was trying to match a trick called the "YOLO flip," invented by the Russian-born eventual gold medalist Iouri "I-Pod" Podladtchikov. But White stumbled on both runs and couldn't gain enough height. He finished fourth. "I'm disappointed," he said. "I hate the fact I nailed it in practice, but it happens. It's hard to be consistent."

Despite that, he remained the face of snowboarding. And his achievements extend far beyond snowboarding and skateboarding. He plays guitar in the band Bad Things, which released its first album in 2014. He is also active in several major charities, such as the Boys and Girls Clubs of America, Make-a-Wish Foundation, and St. Jude's Children's Research Hospital.

Unfortunately, Lindsey Jacobellis—arguably the most

famous female snowboarder in the United States—hasn't enjoyed similar Olympic success. She began snowboard racing in her native Vermont when she was 11 and won a junior world championship within a few years. In 2015, she became the first person to win four world championships in the same event. Her 10 X Games gold medals (as of 2017) are the most for any female athlete in either the winter or summer Games.

Her Olympic misfortunes began at the 2006 Winter Games in Turin, Italy. She held a commanding lead in the final stages of the snowboard cross race. In the second-to-last jump, she grabbed her board and twisted, trying to show off a little. She lost her balance and fell. Though she quickly recovered, she lost too much ground and finished second. "I didn't even think twice," she said. "I was having fun and that's what snowboarding is. I was ahead. I wanted to share with the crowd my enthusiasm. I messed up. It happens." She received harsh treatment from the media. Writers and commentators labeled her a show off and "poster girl for hot-dogging."

Jacobellis dominated her sport during the following four years while waiting for her chance to redeem herself at the Vancouver Olympics in 2010. Unfortunately, during the semifinals, she collided with the eventual winner and didn't finish. Then in Sochi in 2014, she was leading in the semifinals. Coming off a couple of small jumps, she landed awkwardly and crashed. She easily won the "small final," a consolation race, making her officially seventh overall.

"I don't think it has to do with the Olympics," Jacobellis said afterward. "It's just on a fluke of when things work out for me and when they don't." Teammate Faye

A 10-time champion of the X Games snowboard cross, Lindsey Jacobellis has competed in 4 Winter Olympics as of 2018, earning a silver medal in 2006.

Gulini said, "People don't understand how much pressure is put on her. It breaks my heart, because I think it takes the fun out of it for her.... It's a bummer. She deserves more."

She began 2015 by winning the snowboard cross race in both the World Championships and the X Games. Her first move after winning the X Games was rushing over to Eva Samková of the Czech Republic, the 2014 Olympic champion. Samková had crashed. "I just wanted to make sure she was okay," Jacobellis said. "I know what it's like to fall." Asked if she planned to compete in the 2018 Olympics in South Korea, Jacobellis didn't hesitate. "Absolutely," she said. At her fourth Olympics, she came in fourth by only three-hundredths of a second.

Snowboarding Bandwagon

When they're not on the slopes, boarders can keep in touch with their sport through several aspects of pop culture. In Matt Christopher's *Snowboard Champ* (2004), the main character Matt Harper's mother takes a foreign job. As a result, Matt goes to live with his uncle for a year. When he begins boarding, Riley, the school's most popular boy, accuses him of gang membership and doing drugs. Matt's only way of fighting back is on the slopes. Another Christopher title, *Snowboard Showdown* (2007), focuses on the intense rivalry between 12-year-old Freddie and his older brother Dondi. Dondi beats Freddie every time they compete against each other—except in boarding. Freddie cooks up a scheme to use his superior talent on the slope to humiliate Dondi. But his plan puts both of the boys at risk.

Jake Maddox's *Snowboard Duel* (2008), features best friends Hannah and Brian. When Zach—the manager's son at the winter resort where their parents work—arrives on the scene, he forms a boys-only boarding team. Because of this, Brian has to choose between his friend and his favorite sport. In *Half-Pipe Prize* (2010), a character named Tess has to leave her two best friends behind when her family moves. When she returns unexpectedly to compete in the annual boarding championships, Tess is surprised to find that things have changed.

The author/illustrator team of Chris and Robin Lawrie produced the Ridge Riders graphic novel series about mountain bikers. The main character, Slam Duncan, and his friends turn to snowboarding when winter keeps them from biking on their favorite hill. In *Snow Bored* (2007), Slam's good buddy Dozy converts a skateboard into a snowboard. Dozy calls on his newfound skills when a friend's horse is badly injured and he must race to the local veterinarian for help.

Sigmund Brouwer's Short Cuts series includes *Snowboarding ... to the Extreme: Rippin'* (1996). Someone is trying to sabotage Keegan's ski team by stretching wire between two trees on the path they follow down the slope. Then someone targets the ski resort itself and steals their snowboards. To solve the mysteries, Keegan takes up boarding himself. But he soon finds himself in danger, wondering whom to trust.

In Eve Bunting's *Snowboarding on Monster Mountain* (2003), two friends are spending the weekend snowboarding. One girl, Callie, is deathly afraid of heights. Yet her friend Jane wants to keep going higher and higher. Then Jane meets Izzy, who shares her passion for boarding. Will Izzy became Jane's new BFF?

The *Sports Illustrated* Kids Graphic Novel series includes *Snowboard Standoff* (2012) by Scott Ciencin. A member of Team Rogue is hurt just before a big snowboarding competition. Surfer Kai Palakiko offers to try to transfer his water skills to the slopes. He makes rapid progress, but team captain Isaac Foster still has his doubts when the competition gets underway. Ciencin's *Avalanche Freestyle* (2011) sets rich kid Tony Jay against rival Jack in a private mano-a-mano atop Silver Falls Mountain. But an avalanche turns their snowboarding competition into a real-life race for survival.

Older readers are likely to enjoy Justina Chen Headley's *Girl Overboard* (2009). Fifteen-year-old Syrah Chen seems to have everything she needs because of her billionaire father's business success. But her half-siblings loathe her, her best friend is angry with her, and her boyfriend just dumped her. Then a spill off her custom-made board results in a severe knee injury that keeps her from doing the one thing that gave her happiness and peace. She must undergo a long process of recovery and find out who she really is.

Warren Miller began making feature-length films

about skiing in 1950. As head of the company Warren Miller Entertainment, Miller showed the popular films at rented theaters and halls in more than 100 cities. Miller helped fuel the enthusiasm for snowboarding when he began including top boarders as film subjects in 1978. The 2013 film *Ticket to Ride* featured Olympic gold medalist Seth Westcott and longtime pro Rob Kingwill in a segment filmed in a remote part of Alaska. "The snow was stable and the lightest I have ever ridden in Alaska," Kingwill said. "I rode some of the biggest, steepest couloirs of my life while we were filming this year—and we had so many good days in a row, it started to wear on my nerves a little bit!"

Hollywood has also hopped on the snowboarding bandwagon with a number of films. Snowboarding buddies Rick (played by Jason London), Luke (Zach

Galifianakis), Anthony (Flex Alexander), and Pig Pen (Derek Hamilton) love their free-and-easy lifestyle on Alaska's Bull Mountain in the 2001 film *Out Cold*. But when the owner dies, his son wants to sell the mountain resort to a developer. The guys and their friends try to make sure the sale doesn't happen.

In *Shred* (2008), retired pro boarders Max (Dave England) and Eddy the Yeti (Mike Miller) quit their jobs as ski lift operators and start their own school to train up-and-coming boarders. An old rival of theirs, Kingsley Brown (Tom Green), is an executive with a large snowboard manufacturer and head of the National Snowboard Association. He tries to undercut Max and Eddy's efforts and keep their best students out of an important competition. *Shred 2: Revenge of the Boarding School Dropouts* (2009) shows how the young boarders trained by Max and Eddy are living the rock-star lifestyle. But Kingsley Brown isn't through with his meddling.

The fast action of snowboarding makes it a natural fit for video games. Not surprisingly, several feature Shaun White. Released in 2008, *Shaun White Snowboarding* was followed by a version exclusively for the Wii, *Shaun White Snowboarding: Road Trip*. *Shaun White Snowboarding: World Stage* (also for Wii) debuted the following year.

The *Snowboard Supercross* (SSX) franchise is especially noted for its over-the-top tricks. It began in 2000, and the sixth installment was introduced in 2012. GameRankings has consistently given it ratings that surpass 90 percent. Other popular franchise choices include *Amped* and *Cool Boarders*.

Dual Futures

Snowboarding has certainly come a long way since Sherman Poppen's daughters glided gently through their yard more than 50 years ago. It has been characterized by a willingness to take chances, innovate, and make use of the latest trends. Such innovation will certainly continue in the future.

Boards themselves will keep adapting. As a 2014 *TransWorld Business* report notes, "Although most designers will agree that a board's

---

OPPOSITE: Whether carving turns downhill or flying freestyle through the air, snowboarding is a sport that continues to adapt. New designs and technology promise to enhance the experience for years to come.

performance depends on a combination of shape, flex, base profile, and materials, it's clear that shape is getting most of the attention right now.... 'The past few years have been really fun and creative for snowboard shape design,' says Unity's [designer] Peter Wurster. 'Everyone is really trying new ideas. It's a lot more fun to push shape design than it is to push material innovation.'"

Designers will also benefit from emerging in-board computer technology that provides instant motion analysis. Coupled with a greater knowledge of kinesiology, this technology enables instantaneous ride adjustment. Such feedback will help beginners gain confidence much more quickly. It will be especially welcome to boarders as they age but want to continue in the sport. Some experts believe that manufacturers will even develop new board types utilizing on-board technology to provide a

Summer Snowboarding?

The lack of summertime snow isn't an issue for some hard-core enthusiasts. They grab their boards and head for the nearest sand dune. The ride is a little slower, you have to clomp back to the top after every run because there are no chairlifts, and there's always the risk of getting a mouthful of sand during a wipeout. On the other hand, staying warm isn't a problem. You only need a T-shirt and shorts. The most dedicated sandboarders head for Namibia, a country in southwestern Africa. Its dunes—some of which tower more than 1,000 feet (305 m)—are the world's highest. Closer to home, the majority of sites are in Southern California, Arizona, and New Mexico.

smoother ride for these older boarders.

Technology extends into other areas. Some people foresee having boards with their own Internet addresses linked to in-park servers. With the likelihood of increased video capability at these parks, riders will be able to watch themselves perform at the end of the day as they relax back at the lodge. With payment of an additional fee, the video could even be edited to show personal highlights.

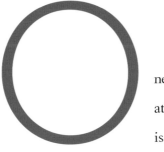ne recent trend seems to take the attitude that if one snowboard is good, two are even better.

The company Dual Snowboards has begun making dual snowboards, one for each foot. Each board is about the size of a cafeteria tray. The primary emphasis is on increased maneuverability, opening up the possibility of new tricks. Some riders may even use them as a form of snowshoe to walk short distances over flat terrain—something that's impossible with full-sized boards.

"Dual Snowboards were invented as a way to bring the best of both skiing and snowboard[ing] together," says CEO Scott Rickett. "You have the fun and ability to ride like a snowboard with comfortable boots and bindings, but now your feet are not locked together, so you have the freedom and mobility of skis without the bulky size and cumbersome poles."

Most people—including company officials themselves—don't see dual snowboards as replacements for traditional full-size snowboards but as complements. "Dual Snowboards make you a better skier and snowboarder," Rickett reasons. "When I put my traditional snowboard on after two hours of riding the Dual boards, I feel like Superman; I ride stronger and harder."

Experts see clothing for snowboarders undergoing significant changes. Currently, riders are encouraged to dress in layers for maximum comfort and flexibility in changing conditions. Manufacturers are placing increasing emphasis on developing ultralight, high-tech apparel that weighs less than a cell phone yet doesn't sacrifice warmth or durability. This apparel may even make layering a thing of the past. Instead, boarders will wear one-piece outfits that automatically regulate body temperature. One example is nano-ceramic fabric, in which contact with natural body heat is enhanced.

Helmets are another source of research. With increasing awareness of the dangers of concussions, manufacturers continue to develop helmets that minimize the problem. They also seek to reduce the overall mass of the helmet and increase ventilation for greater rider comfort.

Many expect goggles of the future to do far more than provide eye protection and screen out the sun's rays. Some goggles are likely to have high-definition cameras and video that can send images directly to a user's cell phone. Others may have built-in displays that measure environmental factors such as altitude and speed and offer Global Positioning System (GPS) access. "There is going to be so much tech in your helmet it's going to be sickening," says mountain guide Mike Hattrup of K2 Skis. "Your goggles and helmet will be like the dashboard of your car. Your beacon, airbag, camera—everything is going to be on your helmet. It's going to be like a Navy SEAL helmet with infrared vision that allows you to see through fog." Access to this information may be initiated by voice commands. For example, you might say, "Give me a trail map and show current snow and weather conditions." That information would then appear on a thin film on your goggles, almost as if it is simply floating in the air in front of you.

ll these developments depend on maintaining the current base of boarders and continuously

adding new enthusiasts. According to *TransWorld Snow-boarding*, "When it comes to creating programs to grow the sport, Burton does more than any other snow sports company to get people of all ages out riding." Burton Riglet Park, for example, offers equipment and instruction specifically aimed at children aged three through six. Burton also provides Learn to Ride (LTR) programs for prospective boarders of all ages at nearly 200 sites nationwide. Those wishing to take boarding to the next level can enroll in the LTR Progressing Rider program. Some programs are geared specifically for women, for those interested in freestyle, and for more advanced boarders who want more expertise in deep powder. It's likely that other manufacturers and ski areas will follow Burton's lead, realizing that nurturing new riders will pay dividends as these people go on to purchase boards,

apparel, and accessories over time.

At some point, boarding may even surpass skiing as the primary winter sport. Whether or not that happens, one thing seems certain. Millions of people will bring their snowboards to the slopes every year, taking advantage of the latest technology yet still enjoying the simple thrill of icy air and carving out fresh powder.

Glossary

adrenaline   a substance produced by the body, often when physically or emotionally stressed, characterized by increased blood flow and heightened excitement

bindings   devices that are fixed to a ski or snowboard to hold a boot in place

couloirs   steep gorges or gullies on the side of a mountain

half-pipes   ramps with two surfaces facing each other that curve inward, equivalent to half of a round pipe

kinesiology   the scientific study of human movement

licensed   granted formal permission to utilize an invention

mano-a-mano   intense competition between two people

patented   gained exclusive rights to manufacture, use, or sell an invention for a set number of years

prototypes   preliminary models of something

slalom   a sporting event along a winding course marked by gates, poles, or other obstacles

slopestyle   a downhill course including obstacles such as rails and jumps; entrants are judged on height, degree of difficulty, originality, and quality of tricks

synthetic   describing a man-made material designed to resemble natural fabrics, such as nylon, rayon, and spandex

Selected Bibliography

Brisick, Jamie. *Have Board, Will Travel: The Definitive History of Surf, Skate, and Snow*. New York: HarperCollins, 2004.

Davis, Steve. *Snowboarding*. Rev. ed. New York: DK, 2000.

Gallagher, Liam. *Snowboarding: Learning to Ride from All-Mountain to Park and Pipe*. Seattle: Mountaineers Books, 2009.

Martin, Danny, and Matt Diehl. *No-Fall Snowboarding: 7 Easy Steps to Safe and Fun Boarding*. New York: Simon & Schuster, 2005.

Masoff, Joy. *Snowboard!: Your Guide to Freeriding, Pipe & Park, Jibbing, Backcountry, Alpine, Boardercross, and More*. Washington, D.C.: National Geographic Society, 2002.

McNab, Neil. *Go Snowboard*. New York: DK, 2006.

Rebagliati, Ross. *Off the Chain: An Insider's History of Snowboarding*. Vancouver, B.C., Canada: Greystone Books, 2009.

Smith, Jim. *The Art of Snowboarding: Kickers, Carving, Half-Pipes, and More*. Camden, Maine: Ragged Mountain Press, 2006.

Websites

TransWorld Snowboarding
https://snowboarding.transworld.net/

This magazine's website provides access to the online version of the publication in addition to photos, videos, current news, a schedule of events, merchandise, and more.

X Games
http://xgames.espn.com/xgames/

The official website of the X Games has schedules, results, videos, photos, and archives of both summer and winter events.

Note: Every effort has been made to ensure that any websites listed above were active at the time of publication. However, because of the nature of the Internet, it is impossible to guarantee that these sites will remain active indefinitely or that their contents will not be altered.

Index